BROOKLYN

TO

MARS

Volume One

MARKUS ALMOND

CONTENTS

INTRODUCTION

Greetings from a bright room in Brooklyn. This is an introduction.

Brooklyn To Mars started as a zine. It happened on a very cold Saturday afternoon. It was snowing outside. I like to take walks in the snow. I try to do it as often as possible. If it's snowing in New York City, odds are I'm out there walking around in it.

My walk that day started like any other. I grabbed my headphones and went outside with my hood pulled over my eyes. But the wind was so harsh and cold that after a while I stepped into a Staples to get warm. I was roaming the aisles for a while until I spotted one of those industrial sized staplers. I picked up the thing and remembered how I used to publish a zine in high school.

If you're not familiar with the term "zine," it's a punk rock thing. It's a Do-It-Yourself thing. Zines are typically self-published, small circulation works of writing, illustrations, comics, photos or whatever the zinester is into. Zines were sort of like a blog before the internet. All you needed was a little imagination and access to a photocopier.

I left the store with that giant stapler, an industrial paper cutter and a brand new typewriter ribbon. I walked home in the snow, ran upstairs to my apartment, dusted off my old typewriter and wrote a few things. That collection of stories and spiritual philosophies became Issue One of Brooklyn To Mars.

It was a crazy idea — to take an ancient yellow typewriter and publish a handmade zine in the age of ebooks and Kindles. But I did it anyway because it felt important. I didn't expect anyone to actually buy one. My goal was to write down some things that I wanted to remember. I wanted a little book I could look back on and re-read when I was stressed or feeling lost.

At the time I was producing an album, running a music licensing company and managing worldwide distribution for an independent record label. I was staring at my computer screen too much. I was on the phone too much. I was doing everything too much. I needed a break from technology. So I sat in front of my typewriter and typed out some things I had been thinking about.

I photocopied the pages and made a cool cover for them. After a while, I asked the local bookstore, Spoonbill & Sugartown if I could sell them on consignment. A nice lady named Susan agreed to take three copies and put them on the magazine rack.

I couldn't believe it when she called me a few days later and asked if I could bring five more. Are you sure? I said. She called again a couple weeks after that and took ten, then twenty more.

Artists and writers started posting quotes on

twitter. Musicians and other amazing people took photos of the zine and posted on instagram. People wanted to know how they could sign up for my mailing list. They wanted to know when the second issue was coming out. I never planned on publishing a second issue. But I enjoyed writing so I kept going.

I am forever thankful for your support. I hope every one of you is inspired to start your own art project, whether it's dancing or drawing or making films or publishing a zine of your own. You can do anything you want in this world. And THAT is what Brooklyn To Mars is about.

What follows is a compilation of Issues 1-5. They've been revised and improved. There is new content and subtle improvements. Because of you, Brooklyn To Mars has taken off further and faster than I ever imagined. Your support has left me very grateful and humbled. I hope you enjoy the collection.

-Markus Almond

ISSUE ONE:
Getting Started

This book is for you, laborer of love, seeker of art, lover of songs, farmer of thoughts or ideas that need to take over the world. I believe that right now, more than ever, anything is possible in your life. You are good at this. You have something truly great to offer and you can make a living doing it. The doors of opportunity are opening in every direction. They open by the thousands. In the Wild West, settlers simply staked out the land they wanted and it was theirs. Many years from now, historians will look back at this point in our history and will marvel with astonishment at the opportunities our generation had. The time to act is now. It has never been this easy. There are no more walls, no more barriers. The gatekeepers have left their hinges swaying. You can do anything you want here. The Wild West has returned.

Concentrate on what you want. Don't let your neighbors or your peers sway you from that beautiful tunnel vision. People will try to talk you out of your dreams for the rest of your life. It's the madmen, the ones who are crazy enough to never let go, that will succeed. You've got to be a little crazy to do something brilliant.

"Your work is to discover your work and then, with all your heart, give yourself to it."
-The Buddha

J.K. Rowling's "Harry Potter" was rejected 12 times before being accepted by a publisher. Record companies told the Beatles, "We don't like your sound," before they were finally signed. Walt Disney was fired by a newspaper editor because he "lacked imagination." Albert Einstein got D's in high school. Michael Jordan was cut from his high school varsity basketball team sophomore year. These people learned how to manage failure so that it became informative and not demoralizing. It took Thomas Edison 1,000 tries to invent the light bulb. "I didn't fail 999 times," he said. "The light bulb was an invention with 1,000 steps." Those who develop a resilient mindset and optimistic attitude will be in good company. They'll have no impediments in life once fear has been replaced by faith. Their diaries will soon be filled with pages of triumph.

"Those heights by great men won and kept were not achieved by sudden flight, but they, while their companions slept, were toiling upward in the night."
    -Longfellow

Now is the time. You will never be younger. You will never be this energetic or this good looking. The universe is yours. Embrace it. Your future is the brightest it's ever been right now - today - not tomorrow. Take the jump. Have faith in the stars and confidence in yourself. Putting things off for another day is the biggest mistake of your life.

You can learn the tricks of any trade and make a decent living for yourself in this country if you have the patience and submissive personality traits instilled in the highest regarded middle managers. Or you can barrel through, and perfect your art never looking back at accomplishments and always improving - ignoring criticism and unflattering press reviews.

The mind is a powerful thing. It has the ability to make us sick, real or imagined. It has the power to make us happy or miserable, excited or anxious, content or trapped. It's all in the way we look at things.

Institutions are outdated. Our schools are flawed. Even the corporate workforce has discarded loyalty, honor and seniority for the cold, hard ruthlessness of bottom barrel payroll hours. Honor everyone around you and always treat people as you'd like to be treated. But with that said, there's no use in putting your future in the hands of corporate marketing plans that may or may not have a line in the budget for your position next year.

Do not hesitate into that great dark night of the unknown. You will be seen through and welcomed on the other side with great illumination and open arms.

Read everything you can about leadership, business and self-development. Our brains run on the software of language. Most people are running outdated or status quo software based on reality television or employee handbooks. Upgrade this middle manager way of thinking and learn everything you can about business development. This will give you the edge and opportunity to break free from the pack.

"Action is the foundational key to all success."
-Pablo Picasso

As you walk through the world you may hear your business associates spewing anxiety and practically shouting at you about tasks they call "urgent." Your loved ones may be in mental paralyses - tangled in thoughts and worries and begging you to take action, or better yet, join in on their emotional anguish. These situations can latch onto your soul and cripple not only your mind but also your physical health and life expectancy. Thankfully, you are a superhero and can walk through war and riots with transforming peace in your heart. Urgency and sorrow will be overshadowed by our unfaltering strength and ability to overcome such manmade anguish that so many fall victim to. Never run from other people's problems. Only look them in the eye until your super powers transform those around you. Your inner peace can change the winter into spring - sprouting tulips from snow as happy geese swim in newly thawed ponds.

Work as hard as you possibly can and then work harder. Never stop.

Honor your soul. You'll be dead before you know it. Maybe even tomorrow. Do you really want to waste your time on earth? You've got a great opportunity ahead of you. I don't know what it is. Only you can know that for sure. Don't doubt yourself. Don't be afraid. Be smart and run for it like a skydiver chases adrenaline.

Most people out there are waiting. They're waiting for something to happen to them. And they talk to each other about waiting for something to happen. But you know what? Nothing ever happens unless you get your ass out there and make it so.

The world isn't gonna slow down for anybody so you've got to know exactly what you want in this life and grab it by the blood-soaked horns and tame the wild beast into a profitable and fulfilling life. Indecision and hesitation will only kill you. You must move fast and you must live and breathe whatever it is that keeps you up at night. Compromise for no one. You will see other parts of your life fall apart and you will have no time to even say goodbye. The only way to true success and grace is to keep your eye on the prize with perfect tunnel vision until the rest of the world fades away.

Successful people do the things that no one else wants to do.

Writing one paragraph is better than not writing at all. Doing five push-ups is better than not doing any. Calling one family member is better than ignoring everybody all together. The hardest part is getting started. If you can conquer that, you'll accomplish a great deal of important things in your life.

We all play different roles sometimes. One night you're headed to bed early knocking on apartment walls for your neighbors to keep it down. And other nights, you're the one setting off fireworks in the apartment hallways, screaming into a broken cell phone and doing shots of tequila out of a boot you found outside.

To my surprise and smiling, tearing, eyes, I've found that this is by far the best time to be alive in the history of artists everywhere. We can have it all. Happiness and autonomy. Financial stability and free time. Everything we need is here for us if we perfect our skills and create something of value. We have access to great sources of information on the internet. The only thing left to do is to take whatever it is that keeps you up at night and perfect it until it's an undeniable force.

"Everything that is really great and inspiring is created by the individual who can labor in freedom."
-Albert Einstein

Drive faster - with the windows down and your eyes on the road with the most intense concentration and deliberation. When the sun goes down you don't notice a change in light but only a drastic change in your self - a mystical shift in your blood stream and body chemistry - the understanding that you are the only person within a hundred miles truly awake and seeing life for exactly what it is - a beautiful list of opportunities and adventures about to unfold.

"All that we are is the result of what we have thought. The mind is everything. What we think we become." -The Buddha

Work as hard as you possibly can and then work harder. Never Stop. I think Thome York once said something like, "If I learned one thing from college it's to keep working no matter how hard things get." Doing what you love and what you're meant to do in life is sometimes stressful and disappointing and hard on the heart. But that's the point. You're supposed to care when things go wrong. If you were working a 9-to-5 job doing whatever your boss told you to do, you'd be half-hearted about every task and wouldn't mind so much when someone else's idea failed. What you're doing will provide you with the highest highs you'll ever know in this life. That wouldn't be possible if you weren't passionate every day of your life. Samuel Johnson once said, "Great works are performed not by strength, but by perseverance." If you take one thing from this book and apply it to your life, let it be perseverance. You must never give up. You must stay strong and focused.

Things were getting hot. The blood was boiling in all of us. Some sought cold alcoholic drinks and bathing in the ocean, others let the sweat roll down their foreheads, arms and fingers into laptop keys, writing away the days too broke to afford air conditioning.

Life, whether you like it or not, moves in fast forward. One day you've got nothing but a wide open future and oodles of time. The next, you're looking back and wishing you would have done more. You can avoid that shooting pain in the soul that comes from constant compromise and ignoring the people that love you. No more excuses. Now is all that matters.

The victims of this world will not soon realize that the key to peace is well within their grasp.

Life can wear and drag on your energy. Things pile up and they take your breath away in an unhelpful manner. They multiply into a laundry list of 'to-dos' that are so long, they need to be printed on butcher paper. And there are always two options for dealing with the time-sucking tasks in front of you - either step up and kick ass, or don't. Sometimes not doing what you're supposed to will free up the energy necessary to accomplish what really matters.

You will not be this young forever. In fact, you're getting older right now. Where do you want to be a year from now? What about five years from now? Do you want to be doing the same thing?

Success is getting your ass out into the world and getting your soul knocked around. And it's about brushing off your jeans and eagerly starting again when you get back off the ground. It's about getting hurt and spit on and then learning how to smile and get stronger. Success is being honest about who you are and what you're capable of and striving constantly to improve. It's about how you really see yourself and it's about letting go of negative thoughts. Success is about living in reality and making right choices.

Every year that passes will never come back. Ask yourself if you want to be where you are today in twelve months. If you're not getting better, you're getting worse. If you're not learning, you're forgetting. If you're not living…well, you know the rest. I highly recommend facing failure and finding a way to thrive. Don't be afraid to rock the boat. Jump off the fucking thing.

Don't take anyone else's word for it. Shine like the rings of Jupiter.

We know that there's something else out there for us. This isn't the only thing we're capable of. We're not afraid of hard work. We're not lazy. But we won't stand for being a new age wage slave and showing up every morning to play a game that doesn't reward our spirituality. Love your work. You deserve to feel alive.

This is your last chance. It's your last chance to ditch the shitty relationship, quit that disgusting habit or chase after that crazy dream. I trust you'll be brave enough to take this opportunity head on and not allow lingering regret to consume your life.

ISSUE TWO:
Minimalism

This issue is dedicated solely to an invaluable tool for artists - minimalism. We don't need the junk in our closets or the clutter in our homes. We don't need to spend all of our money buying things and fixing things. We don't need to spend all of our free time fixing things or cleaning things or organizing things. What we need is simplicity. What we need is more free time and the ability to focus on our art. Issue Two of Brooklyn To Mars explores the benefits of living a simplified and meaningful life.

There is an illusion that has swept and become ingrained in American culture. The illusion is that we need things and income to be happy. This illusion is in front of us every day in the form of advertisements and peer pressure to earn and consume. This illusion is doing our souls and hearts a great disservice and it's time to take a step back and reevaluate. It's time to take a stand and enjoy the meaningful things in life.

This year is your year. You've got the gift now to overcome all your fears and be the person you want to be. There is no pressure here. Things will come together easily and lovely. Don't get wrapped up in the details. Use the words "no thank you" whenever possible and do everything in your power to protect your FLOW. Make no exceptions. Your goal in this world should be to make sure your blood stream is moving at a pleasurable rate at all times. Take away longing and you've got peace. It's time to declutter your home, your heart and your mind. It's time to clear up your schedule, save money and get back to what's really important in your life.

People run on hamster wheels purchasing and accumulating - believing they need to work in corporate offices 70 hours a week in order to buy things that cripple their spirits. When the money comes they spend it. Every dollar spent strengthens the bond between themselves and the need for more money. They live paycheck to paycheck, own the most luxurious things in the world and feel empty inside. The only way out of this cycle is to take a stand against materialism and strive towards independence and autonomy. It's only then that we'll have time for the stars and fresh air again.

Eliminate things that don't add value to your life.

Here's a good place to start: I scanned all of my old polaroids last year. I started to take pictures of things that are dear to me and uploaded the jpgs to Flickr. I recycle the items or sell them online. Every experience I have ever had in my life is being digitalized one-by-one. Everything I've owned for years for sentimental reasons is now showcased and easily accessible in pictures. I honor my things and let them go. I find myself lighter and more confident for whatever the future brings.

"A man is rich in proportion to the number of things he can afford to let alone."
-Henry David Thoreau

Living a simplified life is a tool you can use to free up time, space and energy to do what you really want to do in life. Pursue the pulsating organ in your chest and let go of the rest. Minimalism isn't about getting rid of your stuff, it's about focusing on the things you love about life.

I realize that there are people who depend on their belongings for a sense of identity. I realize there are people who roll their eyes at minimalism because they have dedicated their entire lives to accumulating things. They define themselves by the designer suits they wear. One of the most appealing things about being rich is having all your needs met. But there is a loop-hole to this. If you can diminish your wants and live on less, you're just as powerful as the asshole in the Valentino suit. The only difference is that he is working 60 hour weeks, and you don't have to worry about staining your slacks when you sit on the beach.

It's too often we're bombarded by cmails - typed with neurotic, anxious finger tips - energy drinks flowing through the veins of colleagues as they chase dollars and ignore the urge to collapse by exhaustion. It's time we take a stand and delete those petty emails. It's time we take our lives back and spend time with our soul mates. It's time we put up the away message and get back to living.

Say, "No thank you," to phone calls you're not excited about. Say, "No thank you," to obligations, options and commitments that don't leave you energized and wanting more. Let it go. Let it go. Doing this will only lead to the greatest things possible and happiness for the rest of your days. No longer must we act like trained monkeys, doing what everybody else is doing and looking to each other for reassurance and recognition. Follow bliss and let the Gods determine the result.

"There's only X amount of time.   You can do whatever you want with that time. It's your time."
-Lou Reed

All the physical objects in your life are temporary. You own the stars in the sky as much as you own that sports car or Persian rug. It will all fade away one day, maybe long after you do, but still the fact remains; stressing yourself out in order to own junk is about as intelligent as buying the stars from a gypsy on Canal Street. Those who chase material things or a professional identity will die without knowing themselves.

Get the clutter out of your life.

Your neighbors may look at you funny when they see you tossing perfecting fine items on the street. Friends might worry if you tell them you're getting rid of your car to buy a bike and donating your collection of first-edition beat novels in exchange for a Kindle. But will they be laughing when your expenses and spending habits shrink to a fraction of what they used to be? Will they be laughing when you're the only one on your block that's debt free? Will they be laughing when you launch your own business with zero startup money?

Use minimalism to stay focused. You can be location independent and travel around the world. Learn to live with less and let your business work for you. Don't break your back. Be smart and use resources to your advantage. Fuck the Joneses. Hurtful criticism is best left at its place of inception: in the noggins of misinformed bystanders.

Quit everything in your mind and piece your life back together one thing at a time. Close your eyes and pretend that you quit everything. Pretend you wiped all the responsibilities in your life away. You have a completely blank slate. Keep your eyes closed. What would you add back into your life if you could start from scratch? What would you stop doing forever? Think of each thing in your old life. What would you put back. What would you let go? You don't need to know why. Just follow your gut. When you open your eyes, write down the decisions you made.

"Simplicity is the ultimate sophistication."
-Leonardo da Vinci

Living beyond my means was a big mistake. There were two options: 1) find a job that pays more or 2) something else. I've chosen something else. My journey has just started and I'm not entirely sure where I'm headed. But I can tell you that it has very little to do with money and a lot to do with what I love about life.

I'm beginning to realize how easier things were before I was making any money. Years ago, I had no job, almost no belongings and I squatted in a storage shed. But the few books I had were my favorites and the tiny battery powered stereo was more than enough to lift my spirits. I made a table out of cinder blocks and an old door I dragged out of a dumpster. It held only a manual typewriter and an ashtray. I had everything I needed. Living space per person in the U.S. increased 183% from 1950 to 2000. Do you really want to spend time earning money to pay for space you don't need? Cut your work hours in half and get out of the house.

If you need no recognition and no serious bank account, you can do whatever you love to do, every day for the rest of your life. No strings attached. I am amazed at how little we actually need in this world to live a happy and meaningful life. I am also amazed at how the things we own can actually inhibit and restrict us from feeling happy and doing meaningful things. The more stuff I get rid of, the more I realize I don't need what's left.

Everything is a trade off. Time ticks by and you have to choose. You can't do everything you want to do in life. You have to choose. You have to let some things go.

When you wake in the morning only to get dressed and slug your way to a desk for the next 9 hours, when your eyes remain focused for most of your life on nothing but a rectangular blinking screen, when your greatest enemy is sedentary dullness and the threat of never seeing your sex organs again, it's time to cash in your 401K and make that dream vacation your new life.

What is it that you enjoy more than anything in life? What gives you flow? What can you lose yourself in that makes the hours pass by like minutes? What gives you a feeling of being re-energized rather than drained? Whatever it is my friend, you need to make more time for it. Spend every ounce of your will power on what you love doing, not on paying bills for things you don't need. Hard work is exhilarating if you love what you do. There is no substitute for that feeling. If you don't experience joy in your work, stop what you're doing and go find it.

"Everything should be made as simple as possible, but not simpler." -Albert Einstein

My greatest accomplishment in this world was to mentally and emotionally let go of my accomplishments. I've started donating all of my dress shirts, black slacks and ties to the Good Will in Brooklyn. Let's stop dressing for others. Let's cut our wardrobes so we can fit everything we own in one suit case. Let's stop following the herd of society and only consume what we need. Let's stop comparing ourselves to others. Let's make the change. Let's improve the wardrobes of the homeless and make our poor the best dressed in America.

Start small first. Donate the clothes that don't fit you anymore. Make yourself a promise to empty a drawer today. Once you start to gain momentum, you'll find that minimizing your belongings can provide a great spiritual relief. And once you're a converted minimalist, you'll notice your credit card bills shrinking and your bank account growing. When you let go of junk, you make room for the things that matter. You'll notice that cutting your consumption will have a direct, positive impact on your level of happiness. Cut your work hours and enjoy your short time on this planet. Honor your life. Honor yourself and stop living for the dollar. Your life can be beautiful if you stop spending every waking moment working to buy things you don't need.

Don't keep things for sentimental value. If it means that much to you, take a digital photo of the item and give it away to someone who may actually use it.

The standard of living has tripled since 1959. And what do most people do with this increased standard of living? They work even more hours to buy more stuff. It's time to do the opposite with these American luxuries. Respect your free time. Relax. Increase your happiness for the same amount of stuff. Respectfully decline the offer for overtime. Hang out with your kids or write a novel. Take a month off for volunteer work in South Africa. Or at the very least, sleep better at night and wake up refreshed.

Change can be scary. And fear is a tricky beast. It can come at you from all angles until you're left with nothing but a breathless body and veins that flow quicker than the Passaic River in a flood. The trick is to picture in your mind exactly how you want the situation to end. The answer to all questions will come in the form of peaceful happiness. Run from nothing. Sit in the situation and allow clarity to settle around you until you can see what's happening without restriction or judgment.

"When there is no desire, all things are at peace."
-Lao Tzu

My friends and I used to have this saying, "take it to the river." We all used lived to live together in an apartment on 11th Street. Whenever something went wrong or broke - lamps, typewriters, coffee mugs - we'd get drunk on the Hudson and end up throwing it all in the water. Sometimes even if our things weren't broken - like a shirt we didn't like anymore or a book that wasn't very good - "take it to the river" we would all say. And somewhere along our years of friendships we started applying that little phrase to life itself. Your girlfriend dumped you? Take it to the river. Job not working out? Take it to the river. Feeling stuck, useless or broken? Take it to the fucking river.

Minimalism can be applied not only to your belongings but to your schedule, your work, your relationships and your life. Your schedule is your life. Stop putting things off and start canceling things that leave you feeling drained. DO NOT live one more day with your schedule full of things that don't make you happy. This isn't idealistic. This is common sense. Something that we must always remember as human beings in the world - you can always choose your own destiny and do whatever it is that makes you the happiest. To do otherwise would be a disservice to the people who love you the most.

If you go to sleep exhausted without a feeling of accomplishment, you are doing something incredibly wrong with your life. Living for your next vacation is complete bullshit. If you don't like what you're doing every day, why not change it? Dedicate more time to what excites you. Make sure it's beautiful. Make sure it's something you jump out of bed for in the morning.

When the days bleed into one another and months speed by and feel like a missed road sign, when in the back of your mind you're wondering if you missed your exit because nothing looks quite right around here, when you wake up in the morning knowing that you'll have to put off your dreams for another day, it's time to stop everything. Take the day off, play a record and get your bearings.

If you were forced to start over. If you had to wipe your slate clean and choose the important things, what would you change? What would you stop doing? Where would you put your focus?

The average human lifespan is about 28,000 days. How do you spend your days? We are all INCREDIBLY lucky to still be alive. We could have passed sooner. We could have been gone already. Every day is a gift and you should treat it as such. Have faith in yourself to make the positive changes. Sit still with your heart and follow that bliss. Be brave enough to turn the rest away.

I've got a good feeling about your life now. I really think you're going to make some amazing changes in your life - changes you're going to be thankful for, for years to come. We'll take this journey together. Keep me updated on your art. Let me know how things are progressing and remember to pass what you've learned on to others. We're the richest people on the planet. Our assets far surpass the value of monetary possessions. I hope you find infinite power in art and self-sufficiency.

ISSUE THREE:
Will Power

I'd like to be a little stronger. If we can go to the gym and run on treadmills until we're capable of running a little more, if we can move weights with our arms until we're capable of lifting a little more, what can we do to be stronger in other ways? If I help a frail senior citizen pick up her dropped Metro card in the subway, will I be able to work up the nerve to volunteer in a soup kitchen? If I do that, will I gain the confidence to give an inspirational speech? If I can tell a girl I love her, can I build up the strength to someday be a good father?

This issue is about will power. It's about choosing the habits that you want in your life. It's about having fun and making changes with ease.

If you want something new, go out and find it. It doesn't make you a bad person. There is still honor in choosing the life you wish to live.

I am a firm believer in small steps. One day at a time we get a tiny bit better at what we practice. Will power is finite. Use it wisely.

Work for one year. Just push yourself to work on that project you've been thinking about, every day for a year. If you do it without exception, you'll most likely succeed. You'll also learn a great deal about yourself in the process.

Will power should only be used for emergencies. Instead the focus should be on slowly building good habits. Create routines and use them to leverage your goals. This way you can accomplish great things in your life with minimal effort.

Don't worry about willing yourself to change. Just believe that the change has already taken place.

Picture yourself the way you want to be.

The energy from the universe is flowing through everything. You cannot control it. The word 'stop' does not exist. There is only change. You can guide and bend the energy. You can fly and glide with it. Sometimes it pushes you unpleasantly. But usually it comes like a breeze and can be harnessed and utilized – like the sails of an ancient vessel, cutting through rough waters from the rippling shores of Fiji to the mountains of Alaska.

Don't think about it too much. Forcing a habit can be like trying to swim in quicksand. Let it go. Picture yourself in the future with your problem just a vague memory in the distant past. Go and be happy.

Don't suffocate yourself. You are already free. Try to go from "I can't do that," to "I can do whatever the hell I want but I choose not to do that."

To be good at anything, you have to make a routine of it.

You don't want to keep having to make the same decision over and over again to accomplish something. Make it very easy on yourself. Change the triggers in your environment and stop thinking about it.

Decisions suck your will power quicker than almost anything else. This is why so many couples fight at Ikea. Do everything you can to cut down on the decisions you have to make every day. Make a list of what you need and set a time to go home.

To make a habit of something, you have to be thinking about it all the time. Draw pictures of it. Write love poems about it. On the other hand, if you want to break a habit, you have to ignore it completely. Don't even talk about it. It doesn't exist.

Get a good map of where you are and where you're going. Keep a journal of how you spend your hours. Track your progress. Tell friends what you're up to. Peer pressure can be used to your advantage. I am working on a new novel. I hope you will keep bugging me until it's finished.

If you want to implement a new habit in your life, just believe that it's easy, you've been doing it for years. Don't look at it any other way. Believe it's already a part of you. Believe that it makes you feel incredible. Believe that your life has become happier, healthier and a thousand times more peaceful because of it.

Will power should be thought of as a renewable energy. It should be used selectively and given the opportunity to replenish itself.

As conscious beings, we have a limited supply of self-control. We should be selective about what situations we get ourselves into. An environment that quickly depletes self-control (like an unpleasant workplace or relationship) can have negative affects in every area of our lives. We should rest, replenish, execute and rest again.

It's easy to become an electro junkyard magnet for bullshit. It's easy to get weighed down with all of our work responsibilities, paying bills, and juggling our to-do lists. A lot of shredded metal and engine parts can get stuck up there and weigh us down if we're not careful. Always remember to flip the switch off for a minute or two at the end of the day. Set the wreckage free.

Build yourself a recovery routine. As artists, we can find ourselves being sucked into the void without a way out. This is why so many have succumbed to the drink or worse. We need to tether a line to the rock of reality before we dive into what we love most about this world - because you really can get lost in there if you're not careful. So build a recovery routine. Sex, yoga, meditation, walking your dog, playing with your kids – these are all things that can bring us back to the real world and help us build energy for the next dive. Longevity is a series of short sprints.

The unsuccessful and the successful are only divided by time and the allocation of resources. Don't stifle your resources. Time and energy are the most important things available to you. Let them flourish and carry you to the heavens.

Recovery is a vital part of success. Some of the most successful tennis players in the world are able to slow down their heartbeats as much as 20bpm between points. Their serves, body control and physical techniques can be identical to lesser competitors. But it's their ability to conserve energy that makes them world-class athletes. Recovery routines are essential for having the strength to conquer when the time comes.

Finding rhythm in your life is the difference between riding horseback and walking. You can find momentum in music, exercise, or simply an unwavering routine. There are tricks you can use while building your stamina. The less energy drained while accomplishing your goals, the better.

It's important to cut out all other struggles and uses of will power while trying to make a major change. Figure out what little annoyances set you off and avoid them at all costs. Talk to your loved ones and tell them what's coming. You will be irritable. Give them a heads up and forgive yourself.

May our negative habits be bulldozed into oblivion and given no second chance to lay their foundation ever again.

Sometimes we have to do things we don't want to do. If we avoid them, it would be irresponsible and detrimental in the long run. In times like these it's best to rely on our poise and grace and jump at the opportunity to show the world how useful fears can be once they're tamed like a horse.

Will power is only the engine starter. Confidence is the gasoline to keep things in motion. You've got to be brave enough to love yourself. Don't look down or you will fall.

Think of the people you love and be better for them. Avoid stress and remain centered.

The great thing about breaking habits or building habits or just outsmarting will power in general, is that once you do it once it becomes a lot more fun in the future. Once you figure out that you're capable, once you see that change is possible, things will snowball and your future will become more elastic.

Making a positive change will improve your outlook on life. It will give you confidence and understanding. You'll see that we really do have choices and options and a say in our own future. We can lengthen our life expectancies and brighten the colors of reality.

You can't change who you are but you can change what you do. Don't be scared. Changing one thing in your life won't throw you off balance. You'll feel better soon. Once it's done, you'll be thankful and will wonder why you waited so long.

Don't reward yourself. The change is its own reward. If you see your efforts as something that needs to be rewarded, you're not seeing things correctly.

What if animals had the ability to change their genetic make-up with their minds? For instance what if an elk could overpower a lion just by believing it was possible. "Lion's are fucking scary," one elk says. "Yeah but what if we stopped running and just stuck our hooves right in the bastards eyes," another says. "Do you think that would work?" says the first one. "There's only one way to find out," he says. "I'm tired of running."

I think it's possible with enough time. Scientists have seen adaptations in natural defense mechanisms before. Maybe we just live in a time where the lion is king and a million years from now, the elk will be tearing those fuzzy monsters to shreds. We can change who we are. We can be strong-hoofed, lion-killing, super-elk.

The secret with starting something isn't one of will power at all. It is only to imagine you've been doing the right thing all along. And to never look back, not even once.

There are days when everything seems overwhelming. There are days when nothing feels right and everything seems to be falling apart. Today is not one of those days. And if I come across one of those days again, I intend to give it one swift kick to the nuts.

Writing tip #312: Walk into your writing area without shoes (make sure no shoes are within reach). Take a giant box of thumb tacks and throw them into the air (1000 count box recommended). You should now be sitting in your writing chair with bare feet and surrounded by thumb tacks. Write until the thought of bloody feet becomes more appealing than writing.

I'm just one person. And every living thing in this world has a limited amount of energy and capabilities. We can delude ourselves. It's easy to think we can do anything when our lives are on track to smooth perfection. But our power is limited so the most important thing we can do is choose how we use that power - how we spend our time. The way we spend our days determines how we live our lives and ultimately what we'll be remembered for.

I do the best I can with what I've got and I try not to be too hard on myself.

We'll face our fears together this year. If I fall down, pick me up and I'll do the same for you. Historians will pinpoint the exact moment humanity overcame our shortcomings and evolved to a new courageous state. Like Homo erectus, we'll reach into the burning forest and harness the incredible power of fire – ignoring all instinctive fears for the greater good.

ISSUE FOUR:
Karoshi

The Japanese have a word for death from overwork. It's called Karoshi. Stress from working too much is a problem almost everyone has to deal with. Stress-related disease is something we should all pay more attention to. It's an epidemic in Japan. Young, ambitious businessmen are dropping dead from stress-related heart attacks and strokes. Issue Four of Brooklyn To Mars is about battling Karoshi.

We have goals in life. We have things we'd like to accomplish. But unless we allow our selves to rest and enjoy peace, we will burn out before our masterpiece is set free into the world.

If you ever feel like you're spinning your wheels and getting nowhere, you're probably right. But hidden in that despair are little things that are working. As long as you're making an effort, there are things you're doing right. Get as much feedback as possible and concentrate on the things that are working.

Your strongest asset, the most valuable thing in your possession is your voice. It's your beautiful thoughts and ideas and it's the way you laugh and the way your legs feel when you walk down the sidewalk. Your voice is what people fall in love with and what friends and family will remember after you're gone. Tarnishing your voice is disrespectful to the universe. Of course you will grow and change and become wiser. Your voice will ring out with confidence, experience and wisdom. But remember to take care of yourself and never stifle your voice.

When a person alters his or her voice during a business meeting, or job interview, that person is in essence weakening their tone. You are beautiful when you're honest. Hiding or ignoring your voice will have dire effects on your self-image and inner strength. Karoshi will sneak itself into your body and flood your veins with toxins when you sacrifice yourself for money or social status.

We mustn't give up our ambitions or dreams or desire to do great things in this world. We should run after them with everything we've got. But remember to stop at each rest area and stretch your legs. Remember to turn off the engine and refill your fluids every 3,000 miles.

Exercise enables our minds to let go of stressful thoughts. Exercise strengthens our ability to handle stressful situations and to avoid panic when our heart rate rises. It trains our body to push through difficult situations and to recover effectively, making us stronger than we were when we started. Without respecting our bodies and listening to our physical needs, Karoshi will have the upper hand.

Karoshi loves money. It dangles the carrot of more dollars and promotional advancement every day of your life. Karoshi teems with passion for financial instability. It lashes you in the back over and over again with the whip of financial trouble – screaming about overdue credit cards and bills stacking up quicker than your paychecks arrive. Karoshi looses power when you stop buying things. Karoshi has no defenses against a simplified life. Those who honor people instead of work can defeat it.

How can we get ahead these days when there is an infinite amount of competition and everything you do or say seems to be lost in the clutter and static noise and media popping for attention? I have two tips for this. 1) Be so good that you turn heads. 2) Practice your ass off. This takes an incredible amount of time and effort. Malcolm Gladwell says it takes 10,000 hours. I think it takes longer. But you have to be good and you have to be determined to get better. It will take years and years before you wake up and realize you did what you set out to do. Being stubborn can be a virtue in certain situations. And I believe doing what you love without compromise is one of those situations.

Passion can be addicting, empowering, alluring, & provocative. We will drip with lust for it. It will scream at us in the middle of the night begging us to write down our ideas and make love to the manic possibilities in our heads. We wake up too soon and compulsively check email. We believe we will have a breakthrough soon. This is only a trap. If we forget to rest, if we forget to calm down and disconnect, Karoshi will have the upper hand.

We must fight intelligently and strategically. We must say to ourselves "I'm going to turn my phone off and disconnect from the internet until I feel recharged again." Karoshi won't know what to make of this. Those who forget to rest will be blown away by your energy, vision, thoughtful articulation and focus (all of which can be explained by making an effort to take care of your spirit.)

A fool once said, "To be successful, you have to appear everywhere. You have to have a Twitter account and a Facebook page. You need to be on Pinterest and Tumblr and Youtube and you really should consider doing a weekly podcast or hiring a sky writer to write, 'Follow me on Facebook' over the East River." Do you really need to spend hours upon hours ignoring your family for a screen and driving yourself insane with Google Analytics and your projected trajectory of Twitter followers? No. You need an outlet or two so people can find you. Otherwise, there is no way you have the time or resources to appear everywhere at once. If given the choice between managing one social network well, or being average across many different platforms, have some goddamn sense.

Karoshi thrives on good intentions. It loves that you work to get ahead, and to take care of your family. It smiles when you feel guilty for not being productive. This is why so many people are victims of being overworked. While work is necessary and pleasurable, too much of it will overwhelm and harm us. Work is like eating or having sex. It's possible to take things too far. It's possible to overeat. It's possible to become addicted to sex. And it's certainly common for a person to be overtaken by work until it fills every facet of their lives.

The trick is to work with focus and then rest. Start again with focus and then rest. Kick ass until your email is empty and then don't look at it again for 24 hours. Be the best employee your boss has ever seen and then take a week vacation and turn off your phone.

Don't be pressured by the expectations of others. Just because others in your field are killing themselves doesn't mean you need a stress-related disease as well. We must never be lazy. But more importantly, we must never compromise our voice for the status quo.

I'm not sure I understand why so many people are overworked and too damn tired for living. It's discouraging what they prioritize over life. They'd rather get caught up with a 12-hour workday than go see a sunset on the river. They'd rather catch up on some television than go to a parade. I wonder if they know how short their lives are.

It feels good to laugh. It feels good to do yoga. When my hands are shaking and my eyes are being sucked into the computer screen and I feel like my heart is going to explode, I turn everything off and take a walk. It feels good to meditate. It's great to lay down and read a book. A phone call to a friend helps. I admit I struggle with getting sucked into overworking myself every day. But I also do my best to seek peace, enjoy life and be a positive force in the lives of others.

Not having enough money to pay your bills is one of the most stressful things in the world. It can create a mass panic in the brain. What are these bills? Where did they come from? Do we really need the premium channels? There's a whole beautiful world outside. Do we really need the designer shoes? Are we sure we want to attract people into our lives that judge us by what we're wearing? Are we spending money because we're afraid of what will happen if our bank accounts get too far above zero? Maybe we're rewarding ourselves for all the struggle and stress we endured for that paycheck? We should stop buying so much junk and start cutting down on our workload.

There is a person in your life who loves you. This person loves you with all of their being. They are always on your side and they pray every day that you succeed. You're missing the beauties of life every time you're too busy for this person. You're giving up a little bit of your soul every time you choose work over this person. Love them. Call them now and make them laugh.

Accomplishments are fleeting. Your life will be over in the blink of an eye. If there is a heaven, take some beautiful moments with you to remember there. Don't sit up there thinking, "I sure worked my way up the corporate ladder." Smile and laugh remembering your loved ones and the time you swam in the ocean and the broken umbrella kiss in the rain and the time you taught your child how to juggle. And if there is a heaven, smile without regrets that your life was a piece of art and you treated it as such. May you love in every moment and enjoy the temporary beauty of life.

Try not to put things off. Karoshi will attempt to trick you into thinking there will be more time later. There won't be. Prioritize the good things in life. Schedule relaxation.

Sometimes we feel lost and out of touch and we don't even know why. Sometimes we're working on things we don't care about or feel confused about the things we do care about. I think it's important to not be too hard on ourselves during times like these. We'll get back on track again with a little patience and self-forgiveness.

Take care of the people that love you.

We live in an age where the work never stops coming. Remember the phrase "Going postal?" It started when post office workers started shooting everyone at their workplace. "It's because the mail never stops coming," people said. "It's driving them insane." And now, unfortunately, we all have email accounts and the mail never stops coming. We reply and delete for hours and never have anything to show for it. Put up the away message and remember to take breaks from your screens. Don't go postal.

If you're too tired to shave, if you check your email before you shower, you're running things backwards. If the last thing you see before you go to sleep is a glowing phone, there are loved ones that miss your smiling lips. We must defend against this pressure. If you take a stand, others will follow. If you explain that you need to live a healthy life so that you're better at reaching your goals, you'll blow some minds at the office. May we all eat fresh fruit and take daily yoga breaks after conference calls.

Success is a seductive bitch. She wants to make love and she wants you to pick up the bar tab. When something good happens to our art or our career we get a temporary energy. We get the desire to take things even further. Sucking on the tit of success will leave us hard and wanting more. But success doesn't love you and she won't be there in the morning. The only thing that will last is your morals and your values. Don't be suckered in to the come-hither charm of superficial achievement. It will leave us with a million things, but happiness is not one of them.

I write for flow. I walk for flow. My walks are a religious experience. I put on my headphones and listen to songs that lift me up into the sky. My mind dissolves into a beautiful nothing. My entire focus is on the sensation of New York City pavement under my shoes. Drum beats and angelic voices shoot through my ears and race through my veins. I know when the lights are going to change before the cars do. I step out into traffic when the cross street turns yellow. I am focused and I am in tune to my surroundings. I have no worries and think of nothing but pavement and music.

Has anyone taken into account the long-term effects of forcing ourselves to remain physically inactive? Is the internet so important that we should dedicate our lives to it? Standing desks and office treadmills are an insult. Our bodies still know they're on nothing but a hamster wheel. The orca's fin collapses while held in captivity and the human soul is no different.

Maybe the two most important things you will do today are: 1) laugh. 2) Make someone else laugh. Note: You can do these things at the same time.

The expression 'whatever doesn't kill you only makes you stronger' is complete bullshit. There are things in our past that have scarred us forever. Unless we make positive steps to overcome our failures, we're damaged goods. But it's no problem. One of our mind's greatest tricks is the ability to forget. We forget that our hearts were broken and we love again. We forget the people who left us and open up to the possibility of rejection all over again. If we obsess over the hard times in our lives, we may never be brave enough to fly again.

If you're killing yourself with stress and financial obsession, you're doing it wrong.

Wouldn't it be nice to be a positive force in someone's life? Wouldn't it be exquisite to no longer be preoccupied with worries and self-centered stress? Wouldn't it be beautiful to put our concerns aside and focus for a moment on making someone smile? I think that could change the world. I really do.

Sometimes it's best just to pull over into an empty parking lot and get your head together before you move on to the next town.

I don't believe in tracking our progress too closely. I believe in good intentions and giving our best almost every day. And I say 'almost' because we all have bad days and I don't think we should hold ourselves too closely to rigid rules. It's okay to forgive ourselves for getting off track as long as we steer our space shuttles back on course. The asteroids will challenge us and we'll learn as we go.

Work can be an addiction. It can cause mental illness, obsessive compulsive disorder. And it can kill us from the inside by filling our arteries with yellow plaque. But work can be true and honorable and beautiful. And work can be a force of good in our lives. The choice is ours. We can dance with the job. We can find flow and feel energized at the end of the day. If you leave your job feeling complete, you're at the right place.

You may be wondering why someone like me (who claims to write for artists and entrepreneurs) is this passionate about relaxation. There is a very simple reason for this. If you're too exhausted to smile, you can't do your job well. If you're so stressed you're out of ideas, you can't create anything meaningful. If you're unhealthy or unhappy, you're not the best at your job. First you have to take care of yourself. Then you have to take care of those around you. Then you turn dreams into reality.

I'm thankful that the Japanese have a word for death from overwork. It has such an interesting sound – Karoshi. It rolls off the tongue and it's easy to remember. And I'm glad they call attention to this problem and don't just say people are dying of heart attacks or strokes. It's really wise to bring attention to the fact that work-related stress can end someone's life. I would like to send my love to all of those who have died from Karoshi. My love and thoughts go out to their families. I hope that their deaths will always be remembered. I hope that we can learn from them and honor our time on this earth. Let us take care of each other and enjoy life.

ISSUE FIVE:
Self-Talk

This issue is about noticing the things that hold you back so that you can overcome them. This issue is about breaking down invisible walls. It's about letting go of insecurities and negative self-talk so that you can concentrate on making art. It's about changing the way you think about yourself. This issue is about having the guts to love yourself.

Everyone has different things holding themselves back. Knowing what they are is 90% of the battle. These things are a part of us. Sometimes we don't even realize they're there. Negative thoughts become ingrained in the lense through which we see the world. Pay attention to the next time you think you can't do something. Challenge those thoughts.

Be confident and luck will show up on your doorstep.

As we make little mental shifts in our perspectives, we can create luck and opportunities all around us. We can singlehandedly restructure how we see the world and how we see ourselves. Can you think of one negative thought that you have about yourself? What if you practiced seeing things differently?

Reality is negotiable.

We are born with about 50% of our future already determined. We were placed in an environment with a certain social class. We were given strains of DNA that may lead to sickness or addiction. But the rest of it – the other 50% - we get to choose. We get to choose what we do next. We can blame our parents or our circumstances and explain in great detail how we were never given a fair shot at success. Or we can stop being little bitches and use what we've got to make a difference.

Do you think Mozart ever said, "I wish I could play the piano today but I've got to go mow the lawn?" Do you think Bukowski was worried about upper management at the post office? Successful people with notable talent make positive steps and sacrifices to cultivate their abilities. Their accomplishments were not inherent or God-given. It was all earned through time and dedication. Every talent was nurtured by its beholder. Yes, some were above average in the beginning – but it took ruthless guts to make them great.

I will have shortcomings I may never fully conquer. I will have suffocating fears that I must wake up to every day. But I tango with the beasts until my feet are numb and I will wake up tomorrow to try again.

Bravery isn't for sword fights and war anymore. It's in the boardroom and it's in the speaking engagements and it's in the girl of your dreams at the bar. In the modern world there are no purple hearts and there are no pats on the back for accomplishment. There is only you and the heavens and waking up to yourself in the morning. Every time you step into the discomfort and come through with triumph, you will smile a little brighter and be stronger for whatever's next.

It is a thousand times easier to convince yourself you have nothing to be afraid of, than it is having to use courage to do something. If you can flip your mind and tweak your perspective, you have the power to turn fear into gold.

Improvement isn't about willing yourself to get better. You've got to dedicate yourself to studying your craft. Read more books about what you do. Take a class about what you do. Talk to an expert, ask for feedback, throw yourself out there. Your art needs you to get better. It needs you to perfect your skills. Do the right thing.

Don't worry about how to make a living from your art. Worry about how to make art more often. Worry about freeing up your time so you have the opportunity to get better. This might mean cutting your expenses. This might be taking a job with fewer hours. This might mean giving up drinking with your friends or selling your television. Get your priorities straight. Run towards the fire.

In the past, being successful meant working hard and being smart. In the future, success will be the ability to ignore advertisements and to disconnect from social media long enough to actually create something of value. If you believe in yourself, if you cultivate focus, you will arrive at the finish line of self-sufficiency and abundance.

I read somewhere that the mind's ability to let go of information enables us to learn and remember things that are more important. This is incredible. We are bombarded with information when we walk down the street. If we remembered everything, our minds would be overwhelmed. Learning new things is an incredible gift. But maybe even more incredible is the ability to forget things that aren't helping us. Nobody is perfect and we all have problems. But if we can master the art of forgetting what holds us back, it may help us destroy mental barriers and live a life of strength and happiness.

You've got to let go of the past. And I don't mean ignore it. I mean dive into it head on, pinpoint exactly how it's still holding you back and negatively influencing your decisions. And then toss the memories into the ocean and let the marlin destroy them. We feel guilty. We feel obligated to carry that shit with us. But it's useless. Negative self-talk is worth less than fish food.

I'm sure a lot of people say that you should go to college, earn a certain salary and have children. I realize there is social pressure to do this. But let me just say that societies are absolutely insane. Artists need to carve out their own paths. Ignore the crowds. Slavery, witch-hunts, and brutal wars were all once considered to be completely normal. Please take the status quo with a grain of salt and be brave enough to make your own way.

We are born and walk the earth in cocoons. I don't know why we're in these cocoons but most people live their entire lives without breaking out of their cocoon. They walk the streets and get married in their cocoons. They eat dinner, sip coffee and attend religious services in their cocoons. But it only takes one day and a little determination to punch a hole big enough to let some light in. After that, our imaginations run wild enough to find a way out.

Don't be afraid of your flaws. Bring them to the table for everybody to see. Onlookers will love you for your honesty and courage to be human. It's our embarrassing quirks that make our successes even more interesting.

Let us never mold ourselves in an effort to be loved by others, but rather learn to love ourselves and teach others to do the same.

There is an ocean of peace and strength in your chest. Deep breaths will set you free.

The people we love can do some hurtful things. How we react to those blunders can strengthen or tear apart our souls. In the end, it doesn't matter what happens in the external world. What matters is whether we can live with ourselves after the sun has set and whether we're brave enough to embrace forgiveness in the morning.

See the solution. Instead of viewing yourself as poor, think of yourself as a rich person that is currently underpaid. See yourself as a successful person who has not yet prevailed in the external world. Don't give up on yourself. You are a seed with the potential to sprout into an enormous willow tree. The only thing that could prevent success is if you refuse to sprout and continue to view yourself as only a seed.

We are only people. There is something much bigger than us at work here. If you want to make art, you've got to get out of the way. You can't conceive or contrive the thing. Your only job is to be a vessel and question nothing. Edit later if you must. But when you're in the act of creating, you should be doing as little thinking as possible. The unnamable force will rush like lava on a new planet if you surrender yourself to it.

Meditation can help you spot the thoughts that hold you back. You learn how to observe the mind. You become a well-informed spectator of thoughts. The next time you sell yourself short or miss an opportunity, you can catch this flaw and change as necessary.

Let's not over-analyze. Let's not take on the fool's errand of believing we can figure things out just by concentrating. If we don't have the answers, we'll get our asses out into the world and start poking around. We'll do more lunch dates and ask more questions. We'll put ourselves out there and look for open doors. Nothing can be accomplished with worrying too much.

Making art is like raising a child. It's really not about you. Your art needs fans and admirers to survive. Your art wants to live. It wants a life of its own and it doesn't care about your bullshit. Your art doesn't care if you drink too much, can't keep a job or never learned how to stay in a relationship. Art needs you to be the best vessel you can be. This means constantly acquiring new skills. This means getting out of the way when then the universe opens up and the next project begins to come pouring out of you. Do your job and get out of the way.

Break through your imaginary walls. Most of the dangers in your life are only imaginary. When the Iron Curtain came down in Germany there were entire species of deer that wouldn't cross the places where the border had been in the forest. Generation after generation, the deer wouldn't cross the area where the wall used to be. Don't be like those deer. Walk through the invisible wall.

Our imaginations are the most incredible thing we have. They are magical. We can do anything with the power of our minds.

If you know what you want to do with your life and haven't done it yet, the road to success is very easy. First you look to other people that have accomplished what you would like to do. Then you ask yourself, "What do they do that I'm not doing?" Then you figure out what's holding you back and change it. That last step is where almost everyone gets scared and gives up.

I want to buy land. I want to invest in 10 acres in the middle of nowhere with pines that leave a bed of needles on the ground. I want to go there and meditate and stroll naked and post signs that say, 'No Hunting Allowed.'

Stop holding on. For God's sake move on. There is a mountain to be climbed and you don't get there by talking about the people who aren't in your life anymore. Save them a special space in your heart and carry them to the top with you. Scream their name if you wish. But never go looking for them. They're long gone, man. And you've got work to do.

There are people in your life right now that may soon look to you for help. Do whatever you can to be a capable and generous friend. One day you'll be given the opportunity to help those who've helped you. And I believe it's important that you're strong enough to do so.

You've been through a lot in your life. I know some days it feels like the world has given you a giant pile of shit. It's something I'm sure you wouldn't wish on anyone. But there are other days when you're smiling a wide, childlike smile and you know that everything is going to work out. Let us cultivate more days like these and perceive the world around us the way we wish it to be.

There is no truth, only perspective.

Never forget that the pressures of modern life are only a manmade game. You can take a break whenever you wish. It isn't necessary to stress yourself to the level of those around you. Take nothing as seriously as your universal right to seek peace.

The people we hang out with play a huge part in how we see ourselves. If you wish to take your abilities to the next level, show up where the next level players hang out. Their view of the world will become yours. It's human nature to adapt. You'll improve your skills and increase your talents so that you match your peers.

Have confidence in yourself and let others know that it's okay for them to do the same. Let them know they can believe in you. But most importantly, always exceed their expectations.

Remember that things aren't always what they seem. Intention has incredible powers that cannot be observed or proven by science. If you can change your mind, you can change your life.

I wanted to end this book with something special. Are you ready? Here's a secret about life. We have a lot more influence than most people tend to believe is possible. This is how it works. Are you ready? You can make a change in reality by first making a change in your mind. Then you look for things outside of yourself to validate this reality. After a while, you find so many things to validate the reality in your head, you've created an entire world for yourself where everything makes perfect sense. The problem is that we grow up and we forget we have this power. So most of us create these elaborate stories and lives for ourselves without realizing we're doing it. And those stories aren't always good. If you can get back to that childlike state of imagination and wonder you can change and create anything you'd like in the universe.

Well, that's it. Thank you all so much. The floor is vibrating and ultraviolet is seeping through the curtains. I know what that means. My neighbors are up and I should go to sleep. But I get so excited at night. My headphones blare and there are no distractions. I've got all the time in the world in those moments. And I wouldn't trade the solitude and the clarity for anything. I'd stay there forever. But I know that if I'm not awake in the daytime once in a while, I'd have a whole lot less to write about.

CONCLUSION

Thank you for reading Brooklyn To Mars: Volume One. I really appreciate you taking the time to read it. If you care to read more of my stuff, including Brooklyn To Mars: Volume Two, please sign up for my email newsletter at MarkusAlmond.com.

I would like to thank everyone who gave this book a 5-star review on Amazon. Thank you, Amanda, Robert C. Amann, Holly B., Brandon J. Campell, Nicole Coyle, Patti Edmon, Amanda Eldridge, Justin W. Foust, George Glass, Jacqueline Hang, Kelsey Ives, Walter B. Martens, Brandon Monk, David Paull, Nadia Payan, Matthew Pickle, Joseph Ratliff, The Rosskonian, Sal, Rosco Spears, Russell Wilson, Justin Woods and all you other awesome people. I hope one day we can all have a giant party together.

Thank you for everything.
-Markus Almond

ABOUT THE AUTHOR

Markus Almond is a punk rocker. He spent many years touring and writing music as the lead singer in a punk band. He once played CBGBs in his underwear. You can sometimes still hear his songs on MTV. Markus Almond currently lives in New York City where he now writes books, manages a record label and publishes a magazine.

Made in the USA
Middletown, DE
30 May 2015